JOHN McLAUGHLIN
AND THE MAHAVISHNU ORCHESTRA

Cover Photo: © Redferns

EXCLUSIVELY DISTRIBUTED BY

HAL•LEONARD®

ISBN-13: 978-0-7390-4255-7

"**W**e play music to align the spirit"
-*Traditional Hindu saying*

The Inner Mounting Flame

Birds of Fire

Dear Friends and Music Lovers,

Many times during the past several years people have asked me if and when I am going to publish, in written form the music I have composed, in particular the music performed live and on records by the Mahavishnu Orchestra. With the very kind and able assistance of Roy Perdue, John Curtin and Mark Podolnick to whom I offer much gratitude, this now has become possible.

The music in this book covers the ablums THE INNER MOUNTING FLAME, BIRDS OF FIRE, BETWEEN NOTHINGNESS & ETERNITY and VISIONS OF THE EMERALD BEYOND. Because of the somewhat complex structure of some of the pieces, I have decided to publish a form of "miniature score" instead of the normal "melody-plus-chords" format found in books of this nature. I have used an unorthodox system in writing these scores, but it has proved to be the simplest and most effective way of explaining flow. The use of a miniature score will enable the student to see at a glance what all the instruments are playing simultaneously. It will be particularly useful to read the score while listening to the recordings.

Those who are familiar with my music surely will be aware of the importance of improvisation. The music, when played and improvised upon, forms as a whole a kind of tapestry. The composition forms the vertical threads and the improvisation the horizontal. In fact the tapestry cannot exist without both forms. In addition to the scores, I therefore have shown some of the methods employed by the musicians in their improvisations by including a vocabulary of modes and synthetic modes. Suggestions of what modes to use and where to use them are found below the title of each composition.

Finally, I am including a number of aphorisms which have a particular depth of meaning to me. These have been uttered by great beings who have walked and are walking this earth and who are fully conscious of the supreme significance and power of music.

John McLaughlin

A LOVE SUPREME

I will do all I can to be worthy of Thee O
Lord
Thank you God
Peace
In you all things are possible
We know—God made us so
Keep your eye on God
God is—He always was—He always will be
He is gracious and merciful
Blessed be His name
His way—it is so lovely
It is gracious
It is merciful
Thank you God
One thought can produce millions of
vibrations
And they all go back to God
Everything does
Have no fear—Believe
Thank you God
The Universe has many wonders—God is
all
We are all one in His grace
The fact that we do exist is
acknowledgement of Thee O Lord
God will wash away all our tears

He always has
He always will
Seek him everyday—In all ways seek God
everyday
Let us sing all songs to God
To whom all praise is due
Praise God
No road is an easy one
But they all go back to God
With all we share God
We are all from one thing—The will of God
Thank you God
I have seen God—I have seen ungodly
None can be greater—None can compare to
God
He will remake us
He always has and He always will
It is true—Blessed be His name
Thank you God
God breathes through us so completely
So gently we hardly feel it
Yet it is our everything
ELATION—ELEGANCE—EXALTATION
All from God
Thank you God
Amen

JOHN COLTRANE

MODES

1. Ionian (major scale)

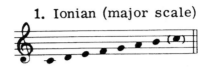

2. Dorian   **3. Phrygian**   **4. Lydian**   **5. Mixolydian**   **6. Aeolian**   **7. Locrian**

As you can see, six additional modes can be derived from the fundamental major mode (Ionian) by starting on each successive step of the fundamental mode. The synthetic fundamental modes are given below. You can derive additional modes from all the synthetic fundamental modes by using the same process of starting on each successive step. I have spelled out all fundamental modes in C for the sake of simplicity, but any mode can start on any pitch. For example, if G# Phrygian is recommended for improvisation, you would play

which is the third mode of E major. Likewise, if the sixth mode of B♭ Double Harmonic is recommended, you would play

Not all of these synthetic modes and their derivatives have been used in this book. However, I have included them for the benefit of the serious music student, because one can find so much hidden within them, particularly in the extraction of their scale-tone chords.

SYNTHETIC MODES

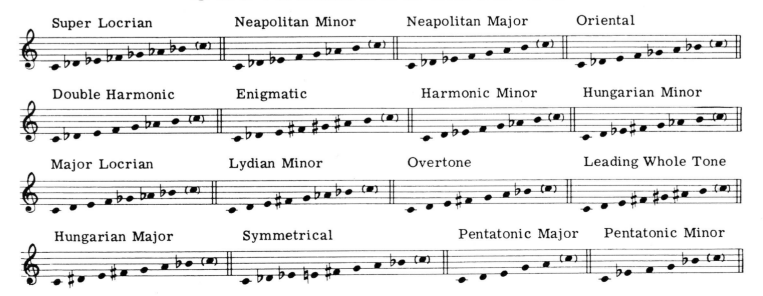

Super Locrian   Neapolitan Minor   Neapolitan Major   Oriental

Double Harmonic   Enigmatic   Harmonic Minor   Hungarian Minor

Major Locrian   Lydian Minor   Overtone   Leading Whole Tone

Hungarian Major   Symmetrical   Pentatonic Major   Pentatonic Minor

CABULARY

REPEATS

Music in repeated sections may be played as many times as desired unless indicated otherwise. Indications may be made either at the beginning of the section (Two times, Five times, etc.) or at the end (, etc.).

In those sections where the number of repetitions is not stated, the directions "Enter 2nd time," "Enter 3rd time," etc. represent the <u>order</u> of entrances. The number of repetitions between each entrance can be unlimited.

THE BOX

The box is a device that uses words to shorten a score. Directions within a box indicate repetitions of previously stated music. After completing all directions within a box go on to the next section of written music.

TUTTI

Sometimes in a repeated section of music the musicians make their entrances one at a time. The term "tutti" in a box or on a D.S. indicates that all musicians enter together.

TRADING

The term "trading" is used to indicate that two or more musicians take turns playing an ad lib solo for a predetermined number of bars. Trading 8's, for example, means that each player in turn plays 8 bars ad lib. Likewise, trading 4's means that each player in turn plays 4 bars ad lib.

DRUM LEGEND

Cymbal
Snare Drum
Tom-Tom
Bass Drum

High Tom-Tom
Middle Tom-Tom
Low Tom-Tom

Unless otherwise indicated, the Cymbal line refers to any kind of cymbal (ride, crash, high-hat, etc.). Notation for one Tom-Tom is written in the second space of the staff. When there are three different Tom-Toms (high, middle and low), the high Tom-Tom is written in the fourth space, the middle Tom-Tom (not Snare Drum) in the third space and the low Tom-Tom in the second space.

Let music of love spread wings of peace over our planet.
No longer pollute our world with poisons of war, poisons of
   greed, poisons of ignorance.
Let all people, all animals, all beings, earth, air and water
   live and embrace in love and peace.
Let music of love heal our little globe.
Let music of love pour out into the universe.
Let music of love rise from our tiny world and join the
   stars of endless milky rivers of light.

ALAN HOVHANESS

(Composed especially for the program "WORLD UNITY: The Song Of The Soul" – October 28, 1975)

DANIEL J. McKENNEY

Meeting of the Spirits

Ad lib solos: F♯ Phrygian or 5th mode of B Harmonic Minor or F♯ Pentatonic Minor

by JOHN McLAUGHLIN

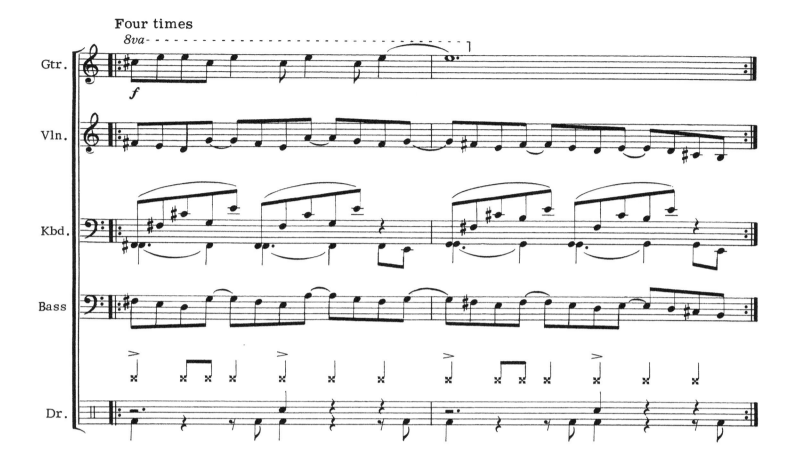

Four times

Dawn

Ad lib solos: Slow section - based on *chord
Fast section - D Pentatonic Minor

by JOHN McLAUGHLIN

*Am11 - A Dorian; C/D - A Dorian; Fmaj7+11 - F Lydian; Eb/F - F Mixolydian; A/G - G Lydian; D - D Ionian.

24

Noonward Race

Ad lib solos: Violin - B Mixolydian
Piano - A Dorian
Guitar - B Mixolydian

by JOHN McLAUGHLIN

* Play G9 chord and intersperse D Dorian.

A Lotus on Irish Streams

by JOHN McLAUGHLIN

* First time Guitar and Violin play melody and Piano plays rhythm ad lib.
  Second time Guitar and Violin improvise on melody and Piano plays rhythm ad lib.
  Third time Guitar and Violin are tacet and Piano improvises on melody over rhythm ad lib.

Vital Transformation

Ad lib solos: F♯ Symmetrical or F♯ Dorian

by JOHN McLAUGHLIN

40

Repeat A Guitar and Keyboard
play as written
Violin solo ad lib
Repeat B

The Dance of Maya

Composition based on E Symmetrical and E Super Locrian
Ad lib solos: E Symmetrical or E Super Locrian or E Dorian

by JOHN McLAUGHLIN

* Third time play Violin melody, sounding as written.

* Last five times superimpose A figure on C.

You Know, You Know

Ad lib solos: E Dorian or E Pentatonic Minor

by JOHN McLAUGHLIN

* 𝄐 is a non-pitched rhythmic accent.

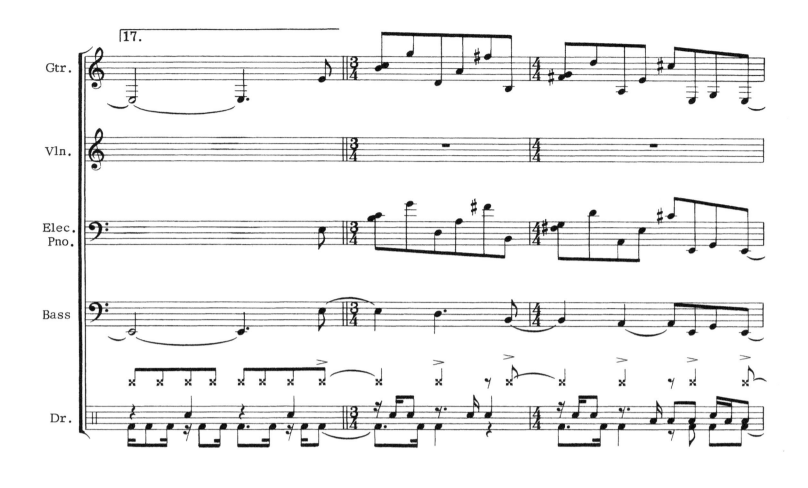

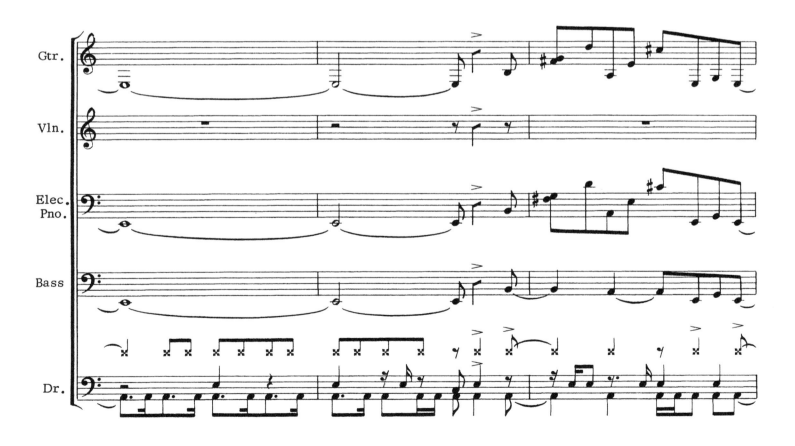

Awakening

Ad lib solos: based on *astrological sign of individual soloist

by JOHN McLAUGHLIN

*According to ancient Egyptian mythology, the corresponding keys (pedals) were assigned to the following astrological signs:

Aries Db	Cancer Ab	Libra D	Capricorn G
Taurus Eb	Leo Bb	Scorpio E	Aquarius A
Gemini F#	Virgo C	Saggitarius F	Pisces B

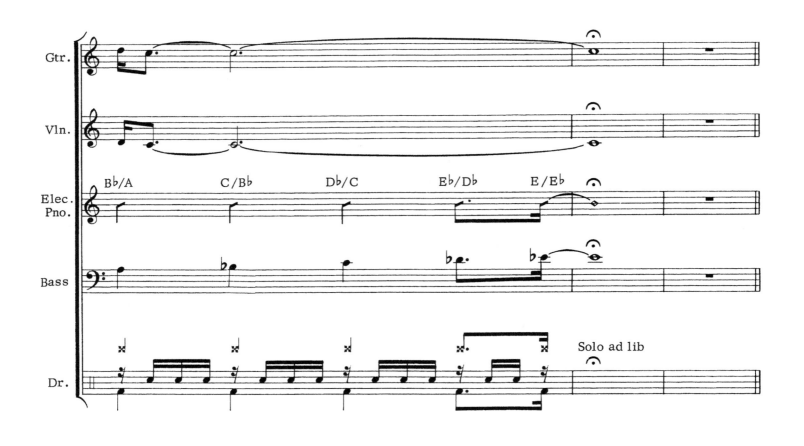

*The modes indicated in [B] are the modes used on the recording; however, the student
is free to base the mode of his solo upon the pedal corresponding to his astrological sign.

The word "spiritual" does not apply to goodness,
Or to wonder-working,
The power of producing miracles,
Or to great intellectual power.
The whole of life in all its aspects is one single music;
And the real spiritual attainment is to tune one's self
To the harmony of this perfect music.

HAZRAT INAYAT KHAN

DANIEL J. McKENNE

Sapphire Bullets of Pure Love

by JOHN McLAUGHLIN

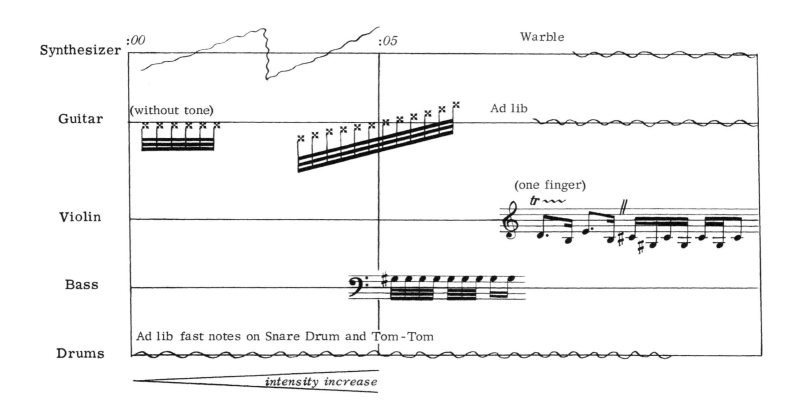

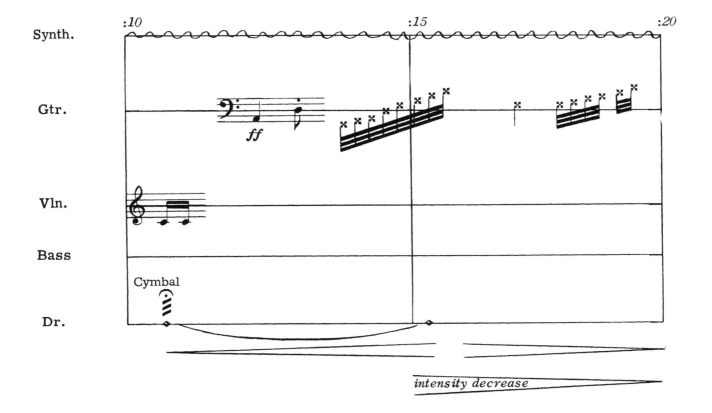

Birds of Fire

Ad lib solos in C : 1st bar - A♭ Super Locrian (E Pentatonic Minor may be interspersed)
                      2nd bar - B♭ Super Locrian (E Pentatonic Minor may be interspersed)

by JOHN McLAUGHLIN

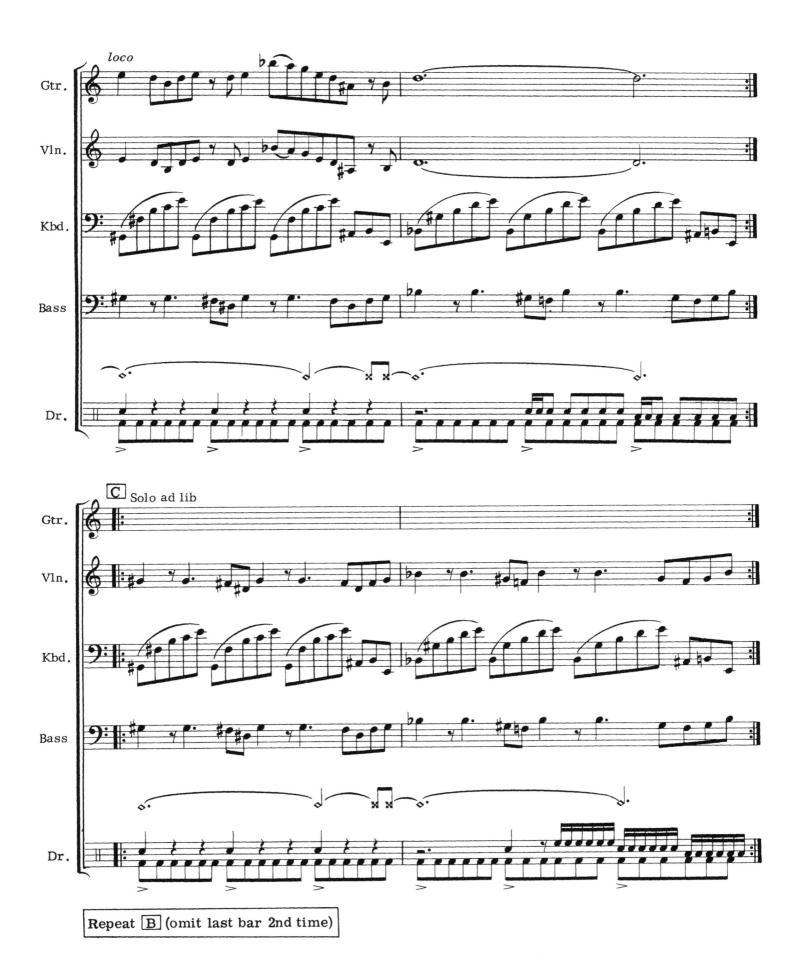

Repeat **B** (omit last bar 2nd time)

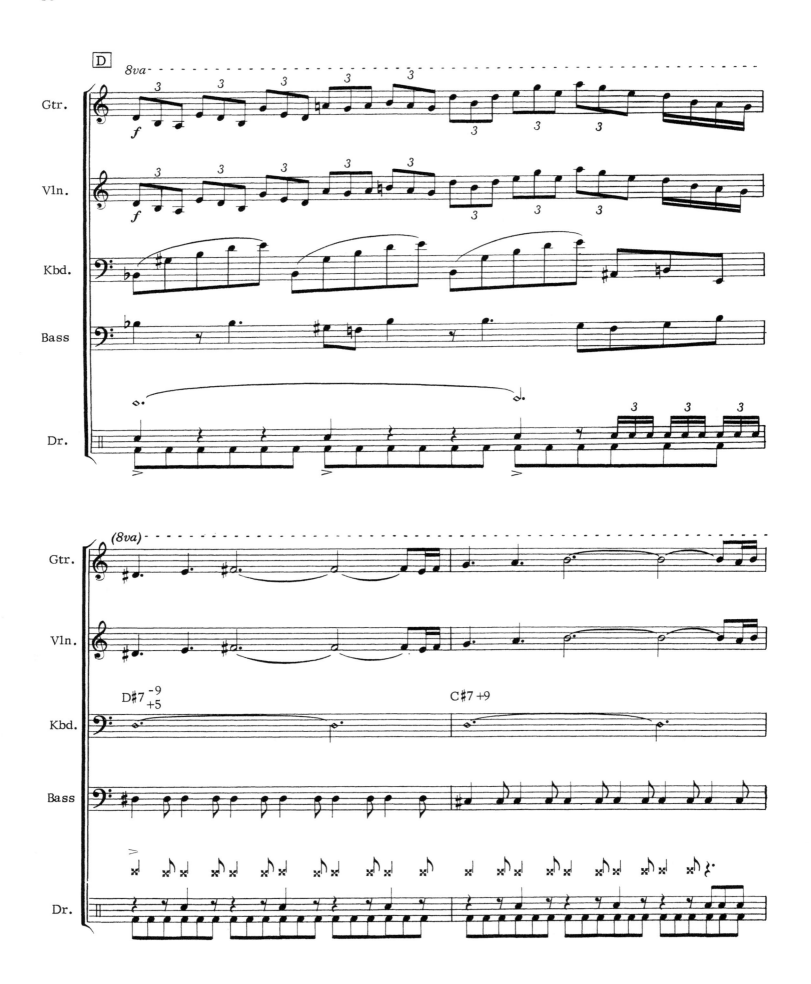

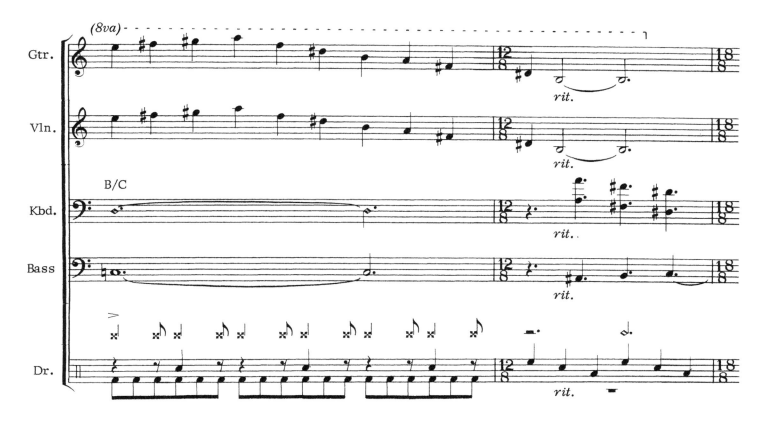

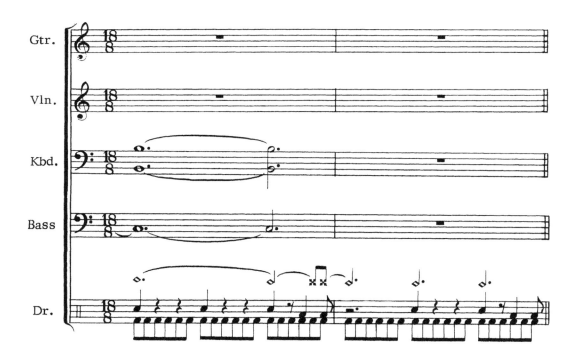

Repeat C Keyboard solo ad lib (Guitar plays written Keyboard notes)
Repeat B (omit last bar 2nd time)
Repeat D
Fade on C Violin solo ad lib (Guitar and Keyboard play written Keyboard notes)

Miles Beyond

Ad lib solos: C Lydian

by JOHN McLAUGHLIN

* In addition to above instrumentation, Synthesizer drones G and D throughout.

64

Repeat [A] Violin (pizz.) and Piano duet ad lib
Rhythm section enters last time
Repeat [B]
Repeat [C] Drum solo ad lib (Guitar doubles Electric Piano; Violin tacet)
Then Guitar solo ad lib (Violin tacet)
Then melody as written
Repeat [D] to Fine

Celestial Terrestial Commuters

Ad lib solos: determined in each bar by first note of Keyboard or Bass part
G - G Overtone
A - A Overtone
D♭ - D♭ Overtone
B♭ - B♭ Overtone

by JOHN McLAUGHLIN

Repeat [A] (tutti) Synthesizer solo ad lib
                       Guitar plays written Keyboard notes; Violin tacet
Repeat [A] (tutti) Guitar and Violin alternate solos ad lib

Thousand Island Park

1st ad lib: F Mixolydian
2nd ad lib: Guitar and Piano - D Super Locrian (Bb pedal)
              Bass - Bb pedal (D Super Locrian may be interspersed)
3rd ad lib: F Phrygian
4th ad lib: same as 2nd

by JOHN McLAUGHLIN

Hope

by JOHN McLAUGHLIN

One Word

Ad lib solos in [B]: G Mixolydian

by JOHN McLAUGHLIN

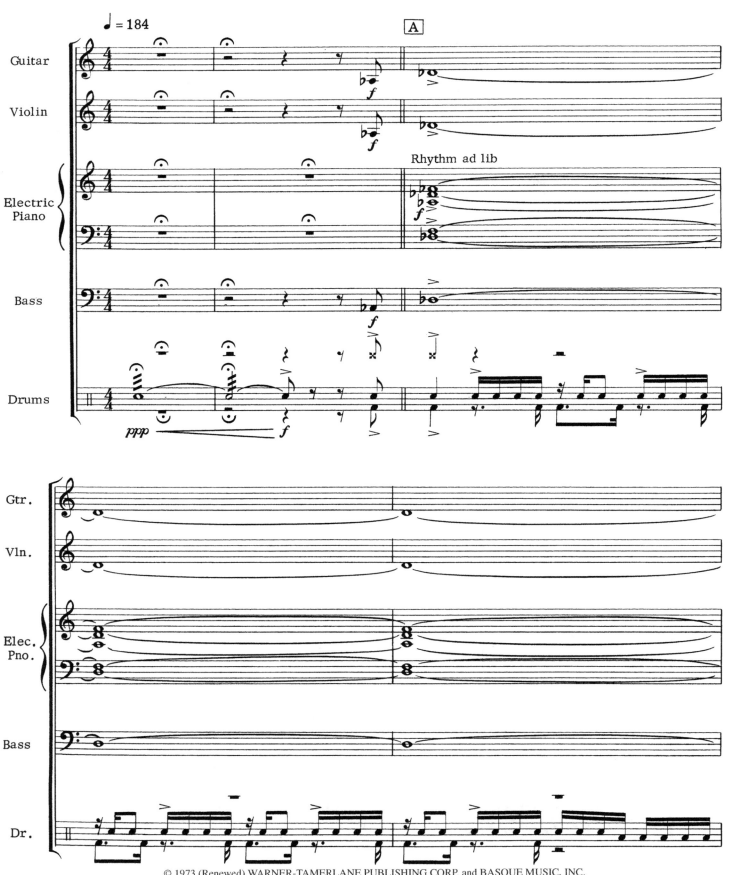

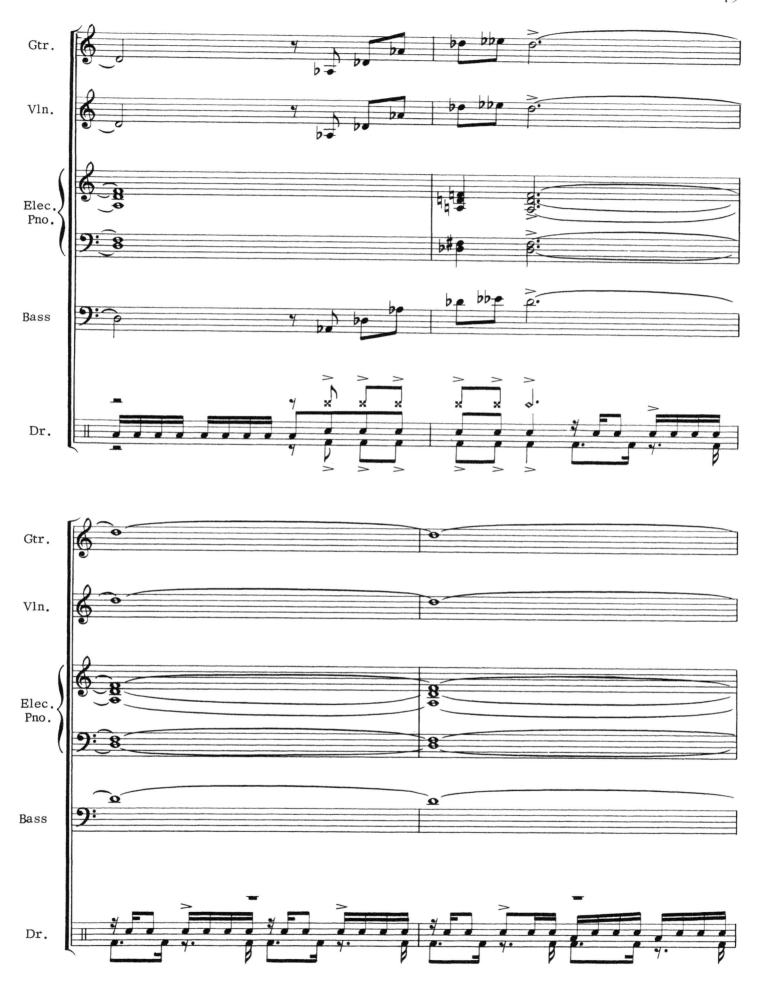

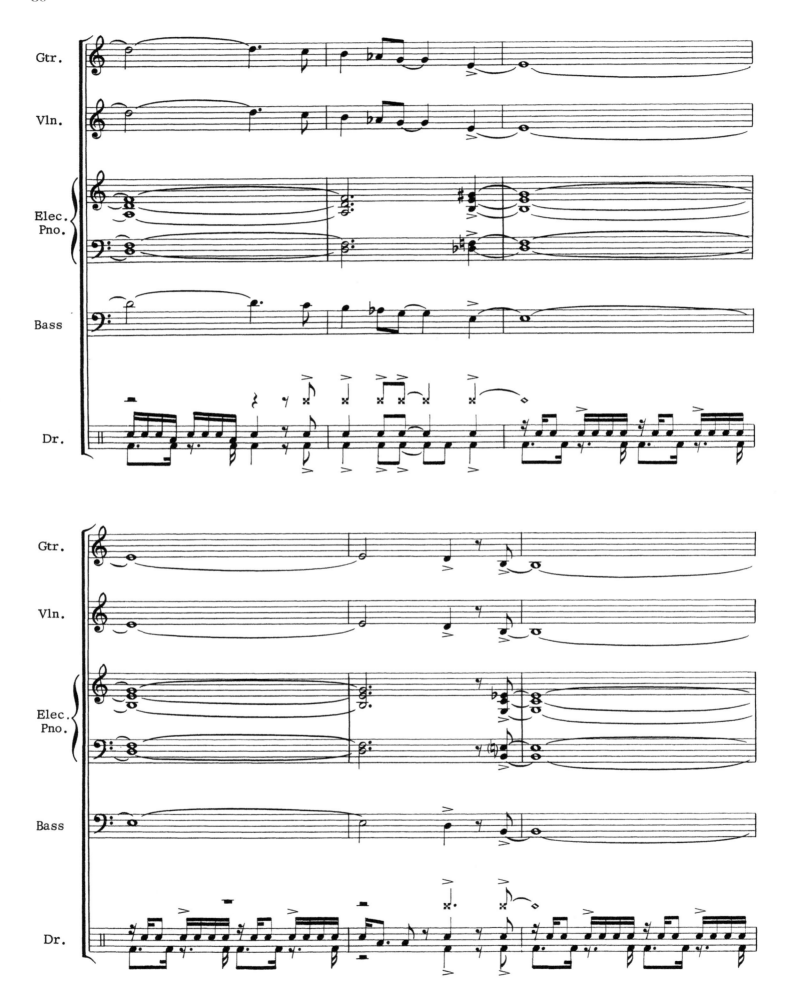

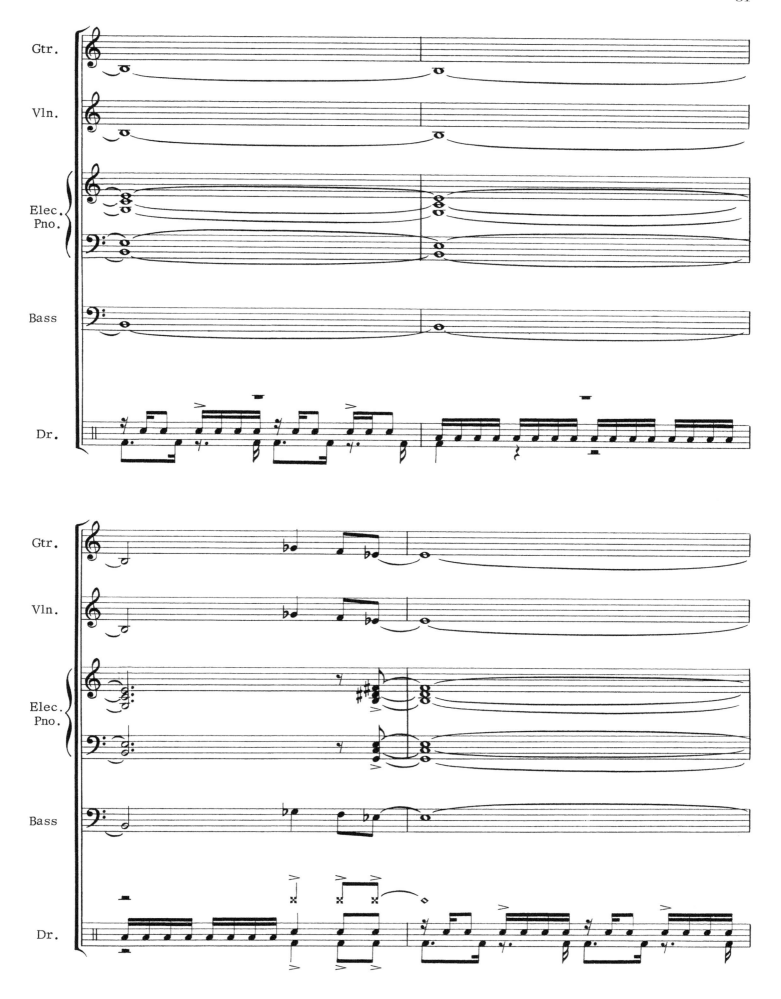

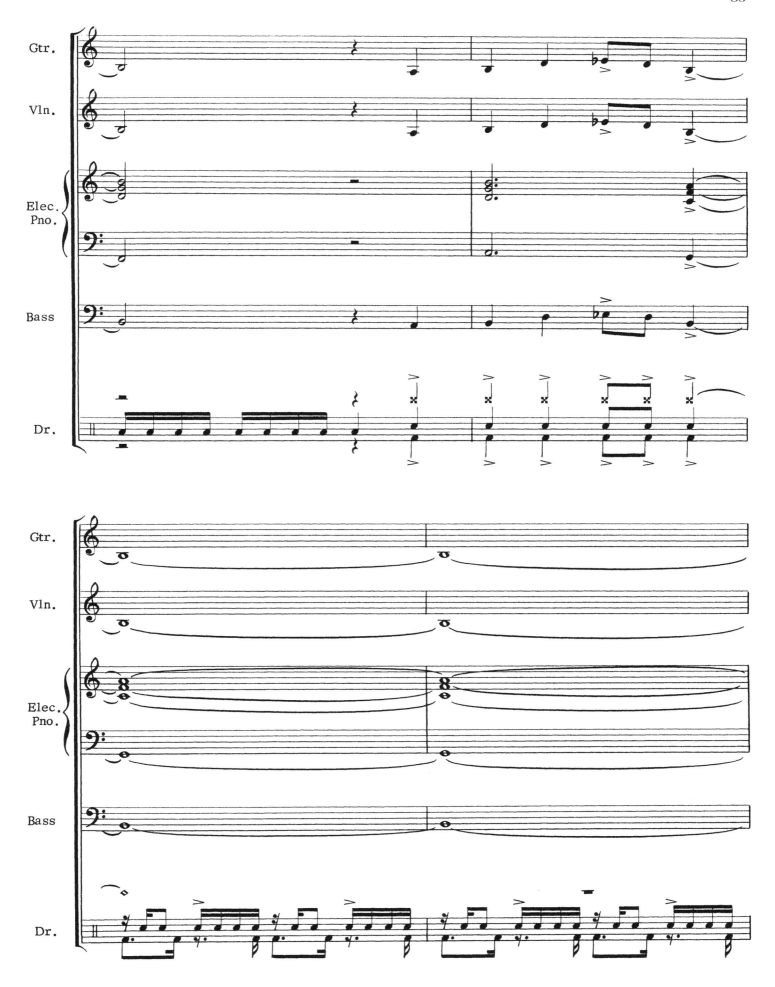

84

C Bass plays solo ad lib (approximately 2½ minutes). Soloist is free to choose mode (A pedal). After Bass solo has begun, Guitar and Piano enter softly ad lib and gradually crescendo. The Guitar, Synthesizer and Violin trade two sets each of 4's, 2's, 1's and ½'s. (Soloists are free to choose modes in trading. It is recommended that each soloist chooses a different mode.) Trading is followed by all three instruments improvising ad lib for six bars. The section ends with a Drum solo (approximately 2 minutes).

A Synthesizer drones A and E throughout (except during Drum solo).

Sanctuary

Ad lib solos: when Bass plays E - B Ionian
when Bass plays C - E Super Locrian
when Bass plays A - A Symmetrical
when Bass plays F♯ - F♯ Lydian

by JOHN McLAUGHLIN

* Snare Drum plays freely, accenting the last beat of every other bar.

Repeat B (except last two bars)
Guitar plays Piano part
Violin plays middle voice of Piano part (as in A)
Keyboard (Synthesizer) plays solo ad lib

Coda

Resolution

by JOHN McLAUGHLIN

* In addition to the above instrumentation a Synthesizer doubles the Violin melody
and a Rhythm Guitar doubles the right hand rhythm of the Piano.

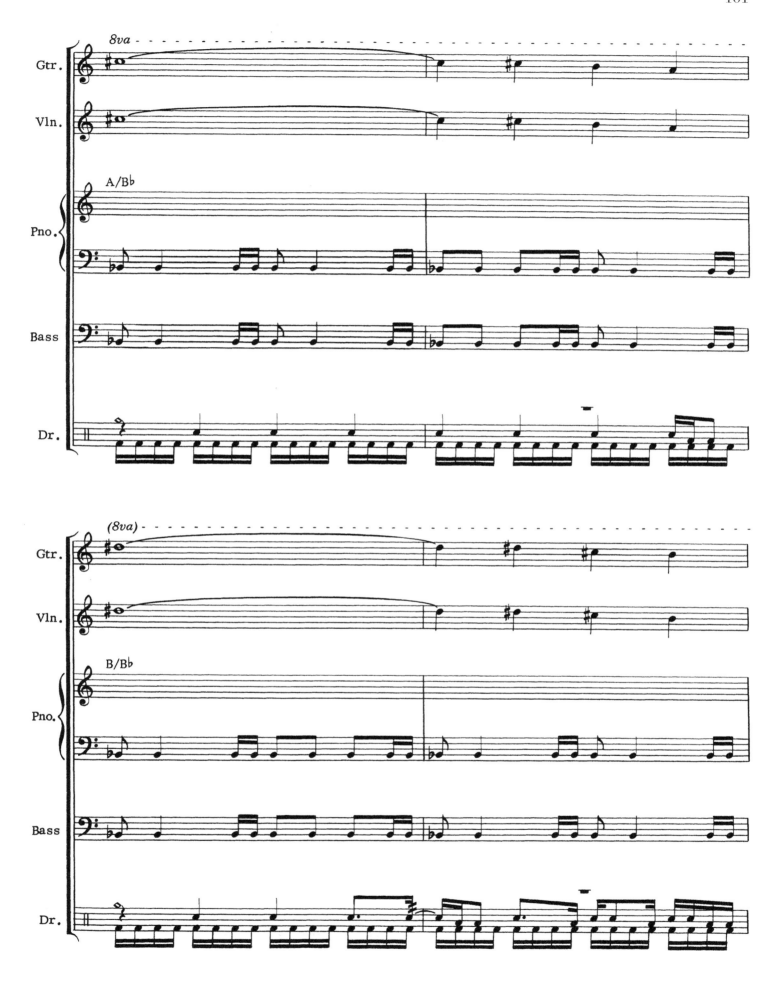

Open Country Joy

Ad lib solos: Fast section - Soloists are free to choose mode (B pedal).
　　　　　　Slow section - D Pentatonic Major

by JOHN McLAUGHLIN

Music must serve a purpose; it must be a part of something larger than itself, a part of humanity.

I am a man first, an artist second. As a man, my first obligation is to the welfare of my fellow men. I will endeavour to meet this obligation through music — the means which God has given me — since it transcends language, politics and national boundaries. My contribution to world peace may be small, but at least I will have given all I can to an ideal I hold sacred.

PABLO CASALS

Lila's Dance

by JOHN McLAUGHLIN

Repeat A (tutti) Violin solo
Repeat B

Repeat B
Repeat A

Eternity's Breath

Words and Music by
JOHN McLAUGHLIN

* On 1st cycle, Organ, Bass, Drums, Violins 1 and 2, and Cello are tacet for four bars.
** Voice, Guitar, Organ, Bass and Drums only on fade.

* The alternate Cello part is written on 2 staves (A and B). The figure
begins on the B line but continues on the A line. At the end of the
figure the sustained high "C" continues on the B line.

* During Violin solo, Guitar plays written notes.

124

Pastoral

Ad lib solos: E Dorian

by JOHN McLAUGHLIN

Repeat A B two times (Guitar and Baritone Violin enter together)
Repeat A (with String Trio)

* Cadenza is based on a selection of modes predetermined by the soloist.

Faith

by JOHN McLAUGHLIN

130

C Guitar cadenza in A

If I Could See

Words and Music by
JOHN McLAUGHLIN

Be Happy

Ad lib solos: G Pentatonic Minor

by JOHN McLAUGHLIN

* Between each statement of melody, Guitar and Violin trade 16's, then 8's, then 4's, then 2's, then 1's for ad lib
solos (melody, Guitar 16, melody, Violin 16, melody, Guitar 8, etc.)
Guitar doubles Bass when not playing solo; Violin tacet when not playing solo; Bass and Drums play above statement throughout.

Earth Ship

Sing 5th, 9th and 14th cycles only

Peace in the heart of the lov - er.
Love in the heart of the joy - ful.
Joy in the heart of the giv - er.

Play 5th, 14th and 18th cycles only

Play 9th and 16th cycles only

Play 5th, 14th and 18th cycles only

Play 9th and 16th cycles only

Play 14th and 16th cycles only

Play 14th and 16th cycles only

* $\boxed{A^2}$ = cycles 5, 9, 14, 16 and 18.
(suggested fade on 18th cycle)

Opus I

by JOHN McLAUGHLIN

On The Way Home To Earth

by JOHN McLAUGHLIN

[A] ♪ = 304

Guitar (with frequency shifter) and Drums play an ad lib duet. After approximately 2½ minutes, the Bass enters while the Guitar (without frequency shifter) and Drums vamp on and around a C pedal.

[B] ♪ = 138

Approximately one minute after entry of the Bass, the orchestra gradually makes its entrance, using the chords spelled out below. The interested student is encouraged to experiment with the use of different instruments playing the voicings. I myself used three strings, four horns (two reeds and two brass), Synthesizer and Tubular Bells.

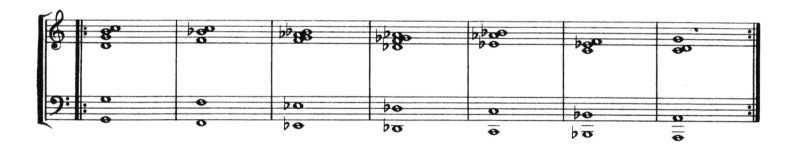

NOTE: The tempos are not related, for when correctly played, one will notice the creation of tension and its release as the slow tempo gradually envelops the fast.

Our sages developed music from time immemorial
For the mind to take shelter in that pure being
Which stands apart from the body and mind as one's true self.
Real music is not for wealth
Not for honours
Or even for the joys of the mind
But as a path for realization and salvation.
This is what I truly feel.

ALI AKBAR KHAN

Dream

Ad lib solos: $\frac{15}{4}$ - E Dorian

$\frac{15}{16}$ - A Dorian

$\frac{15}{8}$ - A Dorian (except last page)

by JOHN McLAUGHLIN

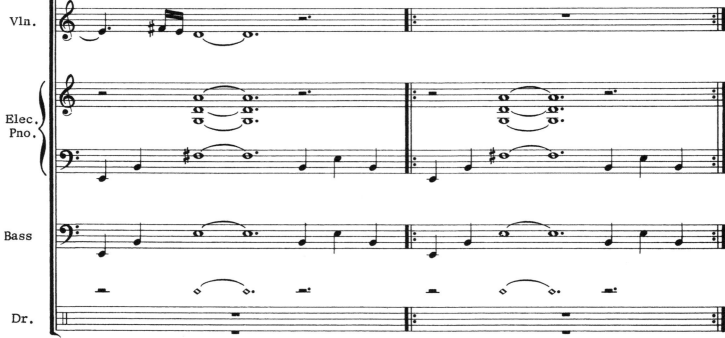

143

* Guitar and Violin ad lib several times (E Dorian), play written notes several times, then ad lib until the end.
Beginning with the last ad lib section all instruments *rit.* and *dim.* and end on the Em9 chord.